Rebellion is the Circle of a Lover's Hands

Rebelión es el giro de manos del amante

November 19, 1993

To Antonio:
  May you always find solace
in the words of your countrymen.

♡ lu

MARTÍN ESPADA

Rebellion Is the Circle of a Lover's Hands

Rebelión es el giro de manos del amante

translation into Spanish by
traducción al español de

Camilo Pérez-Bustillo

and the author
con el autor

CURBSTONE PRESS

Some of these poems have appeared in the following publications:
Agni Review (#28 and #31), Boston University, Boston, MA: "Two
Mexicanos Lynched in Santa Cruz, California, May 3, 1877;" "Nando
Meets Papo;" "La tumba de Buenaventura Roig."
Americas Review (V.18, No.3), Univ. of Houston, Houston, TX: "Portrait
of a Real Hijo de Puta;" "Revolutionary Spanish Lesson;" "The Words
of the Mute are Like Silver Dollars;" "For the Landlord's Repairman,
Since He Asked;" "Shaking Hands With Mongo;" "Colibrí."
Bilingual Review/Revista Bilingüe (V.14, No.3), Arizona State Univ.,
Tempe, AZ: "Rebellion is the Circle of a Lover's Hands;" "Clemente's
Bullets." Copyright *Bilingual Review*; reprinted by permission.
Hanging Loose (#55), Brooklyn, NY: "Cross Plains, Wisconsin;" "The
New Bathroom Policy at English High School."
Minnesota Review (#33), SUNY at Stony Brook, NY: "Niggerlips."
Muleteeth (#1), Boston, MA: "Niggerlips."
Ploughshares (V.16, No.1), Emerson College, Boston, MA:
"The King of Books;" "Jorge the Church Janitor Finally Quits."
River Styx (#30 and #33), St. Louis, MO: "Federico's Ghost;" "Justo
the Painter and the Conquest of Lawrence;" "Bully;" "The Saint
Vincent de Paul Food Pantry Stomp."
*Being América: Essays in Art, Literature and Identity in Latin America
Today* (White Pine Press, Buffalo, NY): "Rebellion is the Circle of a
Lover's Hands;" "Clemente's Bullets."
Speaking to Tomorrow's Leaders: Hispanic Voices, Boston Herald in
Education Program, Boston, MA: "Federico's Ghost;" "Latin Night at
the Pawnshop."

Front cover photograph, "Young Man With Puerto Rican Flag,
Washington, D.C., 1981," by Frank Espada, Puerto Rican
Diaspora Documentary Project, San Francisco, California.

Cover design by Stone Graphics
Printed in the U.S. by BookCrafters

ISBN: 0-915306-95-6
Library of Congress number: 90-52756

distributed by
InBook
P.O. Box 120470
East Haven, CT 06512

published by
CURBSTONE PRESS
321 Jackson Street,
Willimantic, CT 06226

Author's Note:

We have translated this book into Spanish in an effort to communicate with the peoples of Latin America who are the inspiration for many of these poems, as well as to bridge the gap between those Latinos, born in the U.S., who speak English as a primary language, and those more recent immigrants who speak predominantly Spanish.

Muchas gracias to Margorie Agosín, Jack Agüeros, Leo Cabranes, Mireya Pérez-Erdelyí, Cola Franzen, Víctor Rivera, and Tino Villanueva, who critiqued the Spanish translation of the poems; to Rebeca Mingura and Elizabeth McGlynn, who assembled and computerized the manuscript; to Judith Ayer Doyle for designing and printing the cover; to PEN/Revson Fellowship judges Carolyn Forché, Charles Simic, and Daniel Halpern; to Open Voice Award judge Hugh Seidman; and to Amiri Baraka, Cyrus Cassells, Rita Dove, Frank Espada, Katherine Gilbert-Espada, Luis Garden, Askold Melnyczuk, Don Jaíme Pérez, María de la Luz Bautista-Pérez, Andrew Salkey, Juan Sánchez, and Alexander Taylor for their ongoing, generous support of this work.

This work was made possible in part from funds granted to the author by the Charles H. Revson Foundation.

contents/índice

II.   *To Skin the Hands of God*
         Para despellejar las manos de Dios

Dedicado a Clemente Soto Vélez
y
Centli Pérez-Bautista

FOREWORD

"Martín got the stick." That could be this volume's title. It's that clear, like we screaming at the big relay race, "What's that guy's name who just got the stick?"

"Espada," some hip colleague will tell us, "Martín Espada. He gettin' up ain't he?"

Well, he definitely is. He got the baton, and from this view, he is "laying it" as we used to say. "Lay it, Martín!!"

Most of the poems in this book are crafted with one of the most meticulous eyes (& ears, to hear, if it ain't sound it ain't even here) to the created breathing life of contemporary American poetry I've seen de nuevo.

Martín Espada is a young man who should never have to hear the dumb whittle of formalists croaking about "form" (Though undoubtedly he has already). Which to them is something that does not *breathe* or *mean*. Because Martín is, from jump, a "mason" and a half. A verse technologician. The words seem "placed," honed, tightened and rubbed to mint condition. New and Clean!

But what is so gratifying about this work and this poet is that the "technology" is no idle worship of new (usually old) plumbing, all Espada's pipes carry that spark of Ra, Sol (Soul, Alma) *ultimate emotional concern!*

Because Art (created Being) is significant because of the *feelings* (the real life) it can convey. It is the expansiveness of our feelings that are the fuel of evolution. As long as we can feel, we will be alive! When we cannot feel, our "intellectual process" cannot create, since it is merely rationalized feeling.

The focus of much of this volume is the emotional life of Puerto Ricans (especially workers and farmers) in the U.S. and Puerto Rico. And with that the Soc-Pol-Ec reality as well.

Movingly "precise" are his poems on the migrant workers, farm workers in an otherwise industrial setting, also the jíbaro pequeño, small Latino farmers in the U.S. and Latin America.

There is an intensity of feeling here for the Puerto Rican people and culture, as well as the whole span of *Latino* (not *Hispanic* which goes to Spain, as we have *English* Depts. here, and this s'posed to be part of *America*, but *Latino*, as in Latin America!) History, Culture, Life, that is deep-heavy, expressive; poignant, ironic, rollicking, bitter, revolutionary, tragic, by turns. As the poems' I turns, his self is touched by images the work delivers as if he had an amazing Polaroid Eye slung around his neck.

This volume is like one of Trane's *Giant Steps* forward with Espada's work. An Olympic jump so energized the Being has jumped (peeped) feelings — sharp into his own being and the book Being reflects with a luscious, healthy, fleshy, yet critical realist archness a warm human that is the is it is issued out of.

As a lawyer working in housing Espada is a day to day practical advocate of the poor and the homeless. He sees America very close to the way those who are actually disenfranchised see it. He has poems about black and white working people too as well as the declassed petty bourgeois. This adds a wonderful edge of commitment to "be clear," "exact," leaving "not the shadow of a doubt," &c.

Wallace Stevens was VP of an Insurance Co. and we are aware of the quiet distant "real" intellectual fantasies and masques, psychological ambiguities we attend in his work. Martín Espada's work does not necessitate fantasy as its voice, it illuminates reality. Its truth, in its telling, the power and real life force of its re-being (Art) will make new volumes of Espada's still young work as seriously awaited as the next day. The New Soul. Check

Latin Night at the Pawnshop
Chelsea, Massachusetts
Christmas, 1987

The apparition of a salsa band
gleaming in the Liberty Loan
pawnshop window:

16

Golden trumpet,
silver trombone,
congas, maracas, tambourine,
all with price tags dangling
like the city morgue ticket
on a dead man's toe.

Or the title of one poem that summons more life than the ton of sequins and *mierda* that are ejaculated into our threatened lives every media minute by Tío Sham and his Mind Bandits: *The Savior is Abducted In Puerto Rico.* You dig?
"Martín got the stick! Lay it, Martín!"

Amiri Baraka
Newark, Sept. 89

I.

If Only History Were Like Your Hands

Si la historia sólo fuera como tus manos

La Tumba de Buenaventura Roig

for my great-grandfather, died 1941

Buenaventura Roig,
once peasants in the thousands
streamed down hillsides
to witness the great eclipse
of your funeral.
Now your bones have drifted
with the tide of steep grass,
sunken in the chaos of weeds
bent and suffering
like canecutters in the sun.
The drunken caretaker
cannot find the grave,
squinting at your name,
spitting as he stumbles
between the white Christs
with hands raised
sowing their field
of white crosses.

Buenaventura Roig,
in Utuado you built the stone bridge
crushed years later by a river
raving like a forgotten god;
here sweat streaked your face
with the soil of coffee,
the ground where your nephew slept
while rain ruined the family crop,
and his blood flowered like flamboyán
on the white suit of his suicide.

La tumba de Buenaventura Roig

para mi bisabuelo, fallecido en 1941

Buenaventura Roig,
una vez miles de peones
bajaron de las colinas como una cascada
para presenciar el gran eclipse
de tu entierro.
Ahora tus huesos se han ido a la deriva
con la corriente de yerbas brujas empinadas,
hundidos en el caos de malezas
agachadas y sufrientes
como macheteros bajo el sol.
El celador borracho
no halla la tumba,
mirando bizco en búsqueda de tu nombre,
escupiendo al tropezarse
entre Cristos blancos
con manos levantadas
sembrando su campo
de cruces blancas.

Buenaventura Roig,
en Utuado levantaste
el puente de piedra
aplastado años después por un río
desvariado como un dios olvidado;
aquí el sudor rayó tu cara
con tierra cafetalera,
el suelo donde durmió tu sobrino
mientras las lluvias arruinaban la cosecha de la familia,
y la sangre floreció como el flamboyán
en el traje blanco de su suicidio.

Buenaventura Roig,
in the town plaza where you were mayor,
where there once was a bench
with the family name,
you shouted subversion
against occupation armies and sugarcane-patrones
to the jíbaros who swayed
in their bristling dry thicket of straw hats,
who knew bundles and sacks
loaded on the fly-bitten beast
of a man's back.

Buenaventura Roig,
not enough money for a white Christ,
lost now even to the oldest gravedigger,
the one with an English name
descended from the pirates of the coast,
who grabs for a shirt-pocket cigarette
as he remembers your funeral,
a caravan trailing in the distance
of the many years
that cracked the skin around his eyes.

Buenaventura Roig,
we are small among mountains,
and we listen for your voice
in the peasant chorus of five centuries,
waiting for the cloudburst of wild sacred song,
pouring over the crypt-wreckage of graveyard,
over the plaza and the church
where the statue of San Miguel
still chokes the devil with a chain.

Buenaventura Roig,
en la plaza del pueblo del que fuiste alcalde,
donde alguna vez había una banca marcada
con el apellido de la familia,
gritaste subversión
contra ejércitos de ocupación y los patrones de la caña
a los jíbaros que se mecían
entre su seca maleza híspida de pavas,
que bien sabían de bultos y bolsas
cargadas sobre la bestia
de una espalda humana
hostigada por moscas.

Buenaventura Roig,
demasiado poco dinero para un Cristo blanco,
perdido ahora hasta para el sepulturero más anciano,
el de apellido inglés
de ascendencia pirata costeña,
que agarra un cigarillo del bolsillo de su camisa
al recordar tu entierro,
una caravana desvaneciéndose en la distancia
de tantos años
que rajaron la piel alrededor de sus ojos.

Buenaventura Roig,
somos pequeños entre montañas,
y buscamos escuchar tu voz
entre el coro campesino de cinco siglos,
esperando el nubarrón de cantos sagrados salvajes,
derramándose sobre los pabellones arruinados del camposanto,
sobre la plaza y la iglesia
donde la estatua de San Miguel
todavía estrangula al diablo con una cadena.

Rebellion is the Circle of a Lover's Hands
(Pellín and Nina)

for the 50th anniversary
of the Ponce Massacre

The marchers gathered, Nationalists
massed beneath the delicate white balconies
of Marina Street,
and the colonial governor
pronounced the order with patrician calm:
fifty years of family history
says it was Pellín
who dipped a finger
into the bloody soup of his own body
and scratched defiance
in jagged wet letters on the sidewalk.
Around him stormed
the frenzied clattering drumbeat
of machineguns,
the stampede of terrified limbs
and the panicked wail
that rushed babbling
past his dim senses.

Palm Sunday, 1937:
the news
halted the circular motion
of his lover's hands
as she embroidered
the wedding dress.
She nodded, knew
before she was told.

Years later, with another family
in a country of freezing spring rain

Rebelión es el giro de manos del amante
(Pellín y Nina)

para el quincuagésimo aniversario
de la Masacre de Ponce

Los manifestantes se juntaron, Nacionalistas
aglomerados bajo los blancos balcones delicados
de la calle Marina,
y el gobernador colonial
pronunció la orden con calma patricia:
cincuenta años de leyenda familiar
dicen que fue Pellín
quien sumergió un dedo
en la sopa sangrienta de su propio cuerpo
y dibujó su desafío
en letras tortuosas y mojadas sobre la acera.
A su alrededor
el tamborileo enloquecido
de las ametralladoras,
el estampido de brazos y piernas aterrados
y el gemido atormentado
que barría, balbuceando más allá
de sus sentidos que se apagaban.

Domingo de Ramos, 1937:
la noticia
detuvo el movimiento circular
de las manos de su amante
que bordaba
su traje de bodas.
Inclinó la cabeza, sabía
antes de que se lo dijeran.

Años después, con otra familia
en una tierra de lluvia helada primaveral

called Nueva York,
Nina is quietly nervous
when her son speaks of rifles
in a bullhorn shout,
when coffins are again bobbing
on the furious swell of hands and shoulders,
and the whip of nightsticks
brings fresh blood
stinging from the scalp.

But rebellion
is the circle of a lover's hands,
that must keep moving,
always weaving.

llamada Nueva York,
Nina está calladamente nerviosa
cuando su hijo habla de fusiles
a gritos por un altoparlante,
cuando de nuevo los ataúdes se mecen
sobre la onda furiosa de manos y hombros,
y el latigazo de macanas
trae sangre fresca
ardiendo del cabello.

Pero rebelión
es el giro de manos del amante,
incesantemente moviéndose,
siempre tejiendo.

Clemente's Bullets

for Clemente Soto Vélez

Half a century ago,
when the island was stripped of cane
and machetes slashed instead
at the soldiers of empire,
Clemente was a poet in a bow tie
with a gaze
like the mirror of heat on black water,
and the storm-crackle
of his voice
swept the crowds chanting
into the plaza's brilliant noon.
From the podium,
his hands beat the air
like the wings of leashed birds,
orchestrating the heart-rhythm of fists,
the strikers' song.
His words became
the prosecutor's evidence:
"Puerto Rican,
the independence of Puerto Rico
depends on the number of bullets
in your belt."

Sedition, said the general's jury:
six years in prison,
ceilings and floors
huge and gray
as the sides of a battleship
occupying the harbor
of his sleep,
smuggling poems

Las balas de Clemente

para Clemente Soto Vélez

Hace medio siglo,
cuando la isla quedó desnudada de caña
y los macheteros latigaban
a los soldados del imperio,
Clemente era un poeta de corbatín
con una mirada
como el espejo del calor sobre el agua negra,
y la tormenta eléctrica
de su voz
barría las multitudes coreando
en la luz brillante de la plaza al mediodía.
Desde la tribuna,
sus manos golpeaban el aire
como las alas de pájaros atados,
orquestando el ritmo acorazonado de puños,
la canción de los huelguistas.
Sus palabras se tornaron
en las pruebas del fiscal:
"puertorriqueño,
la independencia de Puerto Rico
depende del número de balas
que lleves en tu cintura".

Sedición, dictaminó el jurado del general:
seis años de prisión,
techos y pisos
grandes y grises
como los costados de un buque de guerra
ocupando el puerto
de su sueño,
contrabandeando poemas

fragment by fragment, words like
wooden horses and cows of stone,
during searched and scrutinized visits.
The years' damp
warped the joints of his fingers,
and Clemente learned to breathe
through the clogged lungs
of rasping solitary days.

Since then,
an island of plundered graves and gardens
has drained refugees from the mud,
clay-dark laborers migrating north.
In New York, his long white hair
is winter sky, the smoke of cities
taken by the rebels at last,
as Clemente remembers the language of bullets,
the prosecutor's evidence
that looted his lungs
and abducted the grace of his fingers.

Now when Clemente shouts a poem
his brittle hands are holy,
veined with the lightning of prophecy,
when revolution will race
across the plaza
with a barking of rifles,
and he will awaken
to a morning
in 1936.

fragmento por fragmento, palabras como
caballos de palo y vacas de piedra,
durante visitas rebuscadas y escudriñadas.
La humedad de los años
retorció las articulaciones de sus dedos,
y Clemente aprendió a respirar
por los pulmones congestionados
de días carraspeantes, solitarios.

Desde entonces,
una isla de tumbas y jardines pillados
ha drenado refugiados del lodo,
obreros oscuros como el barro migrando hacia el Norte.
En Nueva York, su largo pelo blanco
es un cielo invernal, el humo de las ciudades
tomadas al fin por los rebeldes,
mientras Clemente recuerda el lenguaje de las balas,
las pruebas del fiscal
que saquearon sus pulmones
y secuestraron la gracia de sus dedos.

Ahora cuando Clemente declama un poema
sus frágiles manos son sagradas,
relámpagos de profecía en sus venas,
cuando la revolución
cruzará la plaza
con el ladrido de fusiles,
y se despertará él
a una mañana
en 1936.

The Savior is Abducted in Puerto Rico

Adjuntas, Puerto Rico, 1985

At a place in the mountains,
where the road skids
into tangled trees
and stacks of rock,
a single white cross leans.

The name has dissolved,
obscured in a century of storms
that asphyxiated shacks
with mud, yanking
the stone vertebrae
from bridges.

On the cross,
the dark absence of Christ
spreads and hangs,
a crucified shadow
where thieves
tore the brass body down,
leaving amputated feet and hands
still nailed,
and the accidental dead
without a guide
on the mountain roads
of the underworld.

Han secuestrado a El Salvador en Puerto Rico

Adjuntas, Puerto Rico, 1985

En un lugar del monte,
donde la carretera se desliza
hacia árboles enredados
y piedras apiladas,
una cruz blanca se inclina.

El nombre se ha disuelto,
oscurecido en un siglo de tormentas
que asfixiaron chozas
con lodo, arrebatando
las vértebras de piedra
de los puentes.

Sobre la cruz,
la oscura ausencia de Cristo
se esparce y cuelga,
una sombra crucificada
donde ladrones
arrancaron el cadáver de latón,
dejando atrás pies y manos amputadas
aún clavadas,
dejando al muerto accidentado
sin guía
por los caminos montañeros
del infierno.

Colibrí

for Katherine, one year later

In Jayuya,
the lizards scatter
like a fleet of green canoes
before the invader.
The Spanish conquered
with iron and words:
"Indio Taíno" for the people
who took life
from the rain
that rushed through trees
like evaporating arrows,
who left the rock carvings
of eyes and mouths
in perfect circles of amazement.

So the hummingbird
was christened "colibrí."
Now the colibrí
darts and bangs
between the white walls
of the hacienda,
a racing Taíno heart
frantic as if hearing
the bellowing god of gunpowder
for the first time.

The colibrí
becomes pure stillness,
seized in the paralysis
of the prey,
when your hands

Colibrí

para Katherine, un año después

En Jayuya,
los lagartijos se dispersan
como una flota de canoas verdes
ante el invasor.
Los españoles conquistaron
con hierro y palabras:
"indio taíno" para el pueblo
que tomaba la vida
de la lluvia
arrojada entre los árboles
como flechas evaporándose,
ellos que dejaron huellas en la roca
de ojos y bocas
en círculos perfectos de espanto.

Y el zumbador
fue bautizado "colibrí".
Ahora el colibrí
se precipita y se estrella
entre los muros blancos
de la hacienda,
un corazón taíno agitado,
frenético como si oyera
el bramido del dios de la pólvora
por primera vez.

El colibrí,
presa paralizada,
cae en la más pura quietud,
cuando tus manos

cup the bird
and lift him
through the red shutters
of the window,
where he disappears
into a paradise of sky,
a nightfall of singing frogs.

If only history
were like your hands.

lo acopan
y lo alzan
por las celosías rojas
de la ventana,
donde se desaparece
en un paraíso celeste,
un anochecer de coquíes.

Si la historia
sólo fuera como tus manos.

Bully

Boston, Massachusetts 1987

In the school auditorium,
the Theodore Roosevelt statue
is nostalgic
for the Spanish-American war,
each fist lonely for a saber
or the reins of anguish-eyed horses,
or a podium to clatter with speeches
glorying in the malaria of conquest.

But now the Roosevelt school
is pronounced Hernández.
Puerto Rico has invaded Roosevelt
with its army of Spanish-singing children
in the hallways,
brown children devouring
the stockpiles of the cafeteria,
children painting Taíno ancestors
that leap naked across murals.

Roosevelt is surrounded
by all the faces
he ever shoved in eugenic spite
and cursed as mongrels, skin of one race,
hair and cheekbones of another.

Once Marines tramped
from the newsreel of his imagination;
now children plot to spray graffiti
in parrot-brilliant colors
across the Victorian mustache
and monocle.

Buscabulla

Boston, Massachusetts 1987

En el auditorio de la escuela,
la estatua de Theodore Roosevelt
siente nostalgia
por la guerra hispanoamericana,
cada puño añorando un sable
o las riendas de caballos de ojos angustiados,
o un podio para craquetear discursos
glorificándose en la malaria de la conquista.

Pero ahora la escuela Roosevelt
más bien se pronuncia Hernández.
Puerto Rico ha invadido a Roosevelt
con su ejército de niños cantando en español
en los pasillos,
niños morenos devorándose
los abastecimientos de la cafetería,
niños pintando antepasados taínos
que saltan desnudos por los murales.

Roosevelt está rodeado
por todas las caras
que él solía agredir con repudio eugénico
y maldecía como mentecatos, piel de una raza,
pelo y pómulos de otra.

Una vez los Marines marcharon
por el noticiario de su imaginación;
ahora los jóvenes conspiran para ponerle grafiti
a su bigote y monóculo victoriano
en brillantes colores
de la cotorra.

Revolutionary Spanish Lesson

Whenever my name
is mispronounced,
I want to buy a toy pistol,
put on dark sunglasses,
push my beret to an angle,
comb my beard to a point,
hijack a busload
of Republican tourists
from Wisconsin,
force them to chant
anti-American slogans
in Spanish,
and wait
for the bilingual SWAT team
to helicopter overhead,
begging me
to be reasonable

Lección revolucionaria de español

Cada vez que pronuncian
mal mi nombre,
quiero comprar una pistola de juguete,
ponerme gafas oscuras,
inclinar mi boina,
peinar mi barba hasta que apunte,
secuestrar una guagua
llena de turistas Republicanos
de Wisconsin,
forzarlos a corear
consignas anti-Americanas
en español,
y esperar
las fuerzas de choque bilingües
sobrevolando en un helicóptero,
rogándome
que sea razonable

Niggerlips

Niggerlips was the high school name
for me.
So called by Douglas
the car mechanic, with green tattoos
on each forearm,
and the choir of round pink faces
that grinned deliciously
from the back row of classrooms,
droned over by teachers
checking attendance too slowly.

Douglas would brag
about cruising his car
near sidewalks of black children
to point an unloaded gun,
to scare niggers
like crows off a tree,
he'd say.

My great-grandfather Luis
was un negrito too,
a shoemaker in the coffee hills
of Puerto Rico, 1900.
The family called him a secret
and kept no photograph.
My father remembers
the childhood white powder
that failed to bleach
his stubborn copper skin,
and the family says
he is still a fly in milk.

Negro Bembón

Negro Bembón es lo que me llamaban
en la secundaria.
Así me decía Douglas,
el mecánico de carros, con sus tatuajes verdes
en cada antebrazo,
y el coro de caras rosadas redondas
que se sonreían con gusto
desde las filas traseras de las aulas,
mientras maestros zumbaban sobre ellas
revisando la asistencia con demasiada lentitud.

Douglas se jactaba
de guiar su auto
cerca de aceras llenas de niños negros
para encañonarlos con un arma descargada,
para asustar negros malditos
como si fueran cuervos espantados
de un árbol,
decía.

Mi bisabuelo Luis
era un negrito también,
un zapatero entre los cafetales
de Puerto Rico, 1900.
La familia lo consideraba un secreto
y no conservaba ninguna foto suya.
Mi padre recuerda
el polvo blanco de la niñez
que no le sirvió para blanquear
su indomable piel cobriza,
y la familia dice
que es aún una mosca en la leche.

So Niggerlips has the mouth
of his great-grandfather,
the song he must have sung
as he pounded the leather and nails,
the heat that courses through copper,
the stubbornness of a fly in milk,
and all you have, Douglas,
is that unloaded gun.

Entonces el Negro Bembón tiene la boca
de su bisabuelo,
la canción que él habrá cantado
al martillar el cuero y los clavos,
el calor que fluye por el cobre,
la terquedad de una mosca en la leche,
y lo único que tienes tú, Douglas,
es esa arma descargada.

Portrait of a Real Hijo de Puta

for Michael

Not the obscenity,
but a real ten year old
son of a whore,
locked out of the apartment
so mamá could return
to the slavery
of her ancestors
who knew the master's burglary
of their bodies at night,
mamá who sleeps
in a pool of clear rum;

and the real hijo de puta poses
with the swim team photograph
at the community center,
bragging fists in the air,
grinning like a cheerleader
with hidden cigarette burns,
a circus strongman
who steals cheese and crackers
from the office
where the door is deliberately
left open.

Retrato de un verdadero hijo de puta

para Michael

No la grosería,
sino literalmente
un hijo de puta de diez años,
entrada sellada a su propio apartamento
para que mamá pudiera retornar
a la esclavitud
de sus antepasados
que sabían del hurto nocturno
de sus cuerpos por el amo,
mamá que duerme
en un charco de ron claro.

Y el verdadero hijo de puta posa
en la foto del equipo de natación
en el centro comunitario,
puños jactantes en el aire,
sonriendo como porrista
con quemaduras secretas de cigarrillo,
hombre fuerte del circo
que se roba queso y galletas
de la oficina
donde se deja la puerta abierta
a propósito.

Cheo Saw an Angel on Division Street

Cheo was a Latin King,
but tomorrow he jumps a bus
for the winter country,
away from the city,
with a vision of the barrio
that will glow
at every gas station
along the smooth night
of the highway.

Cheo saw an angel
on Division Street today:
wandering the block
in the wrong gang colors,
condemned by a sickle of inquisitors,
baptized in gasoline,
purified with a match,
shrieking angel, burning heretic,
brilliant crucifix
thrown through a skylight
on the roof.

And when the chorus of glass
exploded in crescendo,
Cheo heard the angel say:

I am the heat that will flush your face,
I am the sweat of your skin,
I am the one you will pray for,
I am the kiss of the cross.

Cheo vio un ángel en la Division Street

Cheo era un Latin King,
pero mañana agarrará una guagua
rumbo al país del invierno,
lejos de la ciudad,
con una visión del barrio
que brillará
en cada gasolinera
sobre la noche suave
de la carretera.

Hoy Cheo vio un ángel
en la Division Street:
vagaba por la cuadra
en colores de ganga equivocados,
condenado por una hoz de inquisidores,
bautizado en gasolina,
purificado con un fósforo,
ángel aullador, hereje que arde,
crucifijo brillante
tirado por el tragaluz
del techo.

Y cuando el coro de vidrio
estalló en crescendo,
Cheo oyó lo que dijo el ángel:

Yo soy el calor que ruborizará tu cara,
Yo soy el sudor de tu piel,
Yo soy por quien rezarás,
Yo soy el beso de la cruz.

The New Bathroom Policy
at English High School

The boys chatter Spanish
in the bathroom
while the principal
listens from his stall

The only word he recognizes
is his own name
and this constipates him

So he decides
to ban Spanish
in the bathrooms

Now he can relax

Nueva norma para el baño
en la English High School

Los muchachos cacarean español
en el baño
mientras el principal de la escuela
los oye desde el inodoro

La única palabra que reconoce
es su propio nombre
y esto le da estreñimiento

Por tanto decide
prohibir el español
en los baños

Ahora puede relajarse

Willie Fingers

He was born
without fingers,
but could still
shoot a basketball
and win playground bets,
so the hustlers
in East Harlem
called him Willie Fingers;

whenever he was missing
from the block
and someone had to know
"Where's Willie?,"
the hustlers
in East Harlem
always said,
"He's out
growin' fingers."

Willie Dedos

Nació
sin dedos,
pero no obstante aún
podía jugar basketbol
y ganar apuestas callejeras,
y por esto los joseadores
de East Harlem
le llamaban Willie Dedos;

cada vez que se desaparecía
de la cuadra
y alguien tenía que saber
"¿Dónde está Willie?",
los joseadores
de East Harlem
siempre respondían,
"Está
creciendo dedos".

Latin Night at the Pawnshop

Chelsea, Massachusetts
Christmas, 1987

The apparition of a salsa band
gleaming in the Liberty Loan
pawnshop window:

Golden trumpet,
silver trombone,
congas, maracas, tambourine,
all with price tags dangling
like the city morgue ticket
on a dead man's toe.

La Noche Latina en la casa de empeño

Chelsea, Massachusetts
Navidad, 1987

La aparición de una banda de salsa
reluciendo en la ventana
de la casa de empeño Liberty Loan:

trompeta dorada,
trombón de plata,
congas, maracas, pandereta,
todas con sus etiquetas de precio colgando
como la cédula
del dedo gordo de un muerto
en la morgue municipal.

Shaking Hands with Mongo

for Mongo Santamaría

Mongo's open hands:
huge soft palms
that drop the hard seeds
of conga with a thump,
shaken by the god of hurricanes,
raining mambo coconuts
that do not split
even when they hit the sidewalk,
rumbling incantation
in the astonished dancehall
of a city in winter,
sweating in a rush of A-train night,
so that Chano Pozo,
maestro of the drumming Yoruba heart,
howling Manteca in a distant coro,
hears Mongo and yes,
begins to bop
a slow knocking bolero of forgiveness
to the nameless man
who shot his life away
for a bag of tecata
in a Harlem bar
forty years ago

Dándole la mano a Mongo

para Mongo Santamaría

Las manos abiertas de Mongo:
palmas enormes y blandas
que dejan caer las duras semillas
de la conga con un retumbao,
sacudidas por el dios de los huracanes,
lloviendo cocos de mambo
que no se rompen
aún cuando se estrellan contra la acera,
cantos resonando
en la sala de baile atónita
de una ciudad invernal,
sudando en un apuro de noche del tren A,
para que Chano Pozo,
maestro del corazón percusivo Yoruba,
aullando Manteca en un coro distante,
oiga a Mongo y sí,
comience un bolero
lentamente percusivo de perdón
para el hombre sin nombre
que le tiró la vida
por una bolsa de tecata
en un bar de Harlem
hace cuarenta años

Cross Plains, Wisconsin

Blue bandanna
across the forehead,
beard bristling
like a straw broom,
sleeveless T-shirt
of the Puerto Rican flag
with Puerto Rico stamped
across the chest,
a foreign name on the license,
evidence enough
for the cop to announce
that the choice is cash or jail,
that today
the fine for speeding
is exactly
sixty-seven dollars,
and his car
will follow my car
out of town

Cross Plains, Wisconsin

Pañuelo azul
por la frente,
barba encrispada
como una escoba de paja,
camiseta sin mangas
con una bandera boricua
y Puerto Rico impreso
en el pecho,
nombre extranjero en la licencia para manejar,
pruebas suficientes
para que el policía anuncie
que la elección es entre
pago en efectivo o cárcel,
que hoy
la multa por correr a velocidad
es exactamente sesenta y siete dólares,
y que su carro seguirá
el mío
hasta que salga del pueblo

Two Mexicanos Lynched in Santa Cruz, California, May 3, 1877

More than the moment
when forty gringo vigilantes
cheered the rope
that snapped two Mexicanos
into the grimacing sleep of broken necks,

more than the floating corpses,
trussed like cousins of the slaughterhouse,
dangling in the bowed mute humility
of the condemned,

more than the Virgen de Guadalupe
who blesses the brownskinned
and the crucified,
or the guitar-plucking skeletons
they will become
on the Día de los Muertos,

remain the faces of the lynching party:
faded as pennies from 1877, a few stunned
in the blur of execution,
a high-collar boy smirking, some peering
from the shade of bowler hats, but all
crowding into the photograph.

Dos mexicanos linchados en Santa Cruz, California, 3 de mayo, 1877

Más que el momento
cuando cuarenta gringos delincuentes
incitaron a la soga
que jaló a dos mexicanos hasta lanzarlos
al sueño de muecas de los desnucados,

más que los cadáveres flotando,
atados como primos del matadero,
suspendidos en la muda humildad
agachada de los condenados,

más que la Virgen de Guadalupe
que bendice a los de piel morena
y a los crucificados,
o a las calaveras guitarristas
en que se convertirán
en el Día de los Muertos,

perduran las caras de los linchadores:
descoloridas como monedas de 1877, unos pocos aturdidos
en el acto borroso de la ejecución,
el muchacho de cuello alto sonriéndose maliciosamente,
algunos asomándose desde la media luz
de sus sombreros hongos, pero todos
amontonándose para caber en la fotografía.

Sophie's Amulet

for Debra of the Sac and Fox, 1990

Kansas is a whitewashed trailer,
light sharp as the splintered flask
of childhood, that shocked
bubble of blood on the finger.
All remembered when grandmother Sophie
mails a necklace:
blue stones and beaded pouch
for wearing at the pow wow,
for stepping in the great astronomy
of the circle that dances and drums.

An amulet hidden in the pouch:
a gold token for one year sober
at Alcoholics Anonymous,
coin at the core
of a praying fist.

Blessed against liquor and the sellers of liquor,
Sophie's granddaughter dances,
shuffles in a memory of horses,
the shawl's wing, the drum's quake, hard feet
not yet bones for the anthropologist.

El amuleto de Sophie

para Debra de los indígenas Sac y Fox, 1990

Kansas es una casa rodante pintada de blanco,
luz aguda como el frasco astillado
de la niñez, esa burbuja
atónita de sangre sobre el dedo.

Todo recordado cuando la abuela Sophie
envía un collar:
piedras azules y bolsita de cuentas
para ponerse en el pow wow,
para sus pasos dentro de la gran astronomía
del círculo que danza y percuta.

Un amuleto ocultado en la bolsita:
la prenda de oro por un año sobrio
en Alcohólicos Anónimos,
la moneda al corazón
de un puño rezador.

Amparada contra el licor y los traficantes de licor,
la nieta de Sophie danza,
pasos arrastrados evocando la memoria de caballos,
el ala del chal, el seísmo del tambor, pies duros
sin ser aún huesos para el antropólogo.

A Taste for Silk and Black Servants

Your taste
for delicate desserts, silk
and black servants back home,
your money
from the bank manager father
in Johannesburg, where
you cheerfully defied boycotts
to return every Christmas,
your Boer privilege
of receiving mail from home
unopened by the authorities
who scrutinize the anonymous mimeographs
of opposition poets,

your lover in the social register
who married a woman
you called a peasant,
your one black friend
from Harvard
you told everyone about,
your affected accent
and your academic credentials,
your complexion
kept bright with jars of skin cream,

all meant less
than the moment, one night,
when the riots in South Africa
flashed on the television news
and you stepped wordlessly
from the room.

Un gusto por la seda y sirvientes negros

Tu gusto
por postres delicados, la seda
y sirvientes negros en casa,
tu dinero
enviado por el padre gerente banquero
en Johannesburg, donde
jubilosamente desafiabas el boicoteo
para irte de visita cada Navidad,
tu privilegio Boer
de recibir correo de allá
sin ser abierto por las autoridades
que escudriñan los textos mimeografiados
de poetas opositores,

tu amante del registro social
que se casó con una mujer
que llamaste "campesina",
tu único amigo negro
de Harvard
sobre el cual le contabas a todo el mundo,
tu acento exagerado
y tus credenciales académicas,
tu tez
pulida por tarros de crema para la piel,

todo esto significaba menos
que el momento,
una noche,
cuando el levantamiento en Sur Africa
se destelló del noticiero televisado
y tú te saliste del cuarto
sin palabras.

The King of Books

for Camilo Pérez-Bustillo

The books traveled with Camilo
everywhere, like wrinkled duendes
whispering advice.
The fortuneteller clawed his palm
and warned him
about El Salvador,
where the guards
search for books at the border,
plucking at pages
like the pockets of a bearded subversive.

The books were bandits,
bootlegging illicit words
like Che and insurrection.
For the books,
a rifle jabbed in his spine;
for the books,
an elbow pressed against the chin;
for the books,
electrical wires slowly waving,
branches of cruel sparks.

And the captain in camouflage
tried to instruct him
with a wall-hard smack
and rational fascist philosophy;
the guards worked to convince him,
propping him on the cot
with the same interrogation repeated
till morning slipped into the cell
and spread across the floor unnoticed;
the Marines fought to persuade him

El Rey de los Libros

para Camilo Pérez-Bustillo

Los libros viajaban con Camilo
por todas partes, como duendes arrugados
susurrándole consejos.
La adivina le arañó la palma
y le previno
sobre El Salvador,
donde los guardias
revisan en búsqueda de libros en la frontera,
desplumando páginas
como los bolsillos de un barbudo subversivo.

Los libros eran bandidos,
contrabandeando palabras ilícitas
como el Che e insurrección.
Por los libros,
un fusil en su espina dorsal;
por los libros,
un codo contra su garganta;
por los libros,
cables eléctricos meciéndose despacio,
ramas de chispas crueles.

Y el capitán en camuflaje
trató de instruirlo
con un golpe seco contra la pared
y filosofía fascista racional;
los guardias trabajaron para convencerlo,
recostándolo sobre el catre
con la misma interrogación repetida
hasta que la mañana se deslizó por la celda
y se esparció por el suelo inadvertida;
los Marines lucharon para persuadirlo

by stern quiet in the jeep,
dropping him marooned
without money or books
at the border.

He was not persuaded.
In his apartment books breed,
an infestation of books,
piling, spilling,
a horde of printed words like grasshoppers
blackening the nightmares
of treasury police and army captains
in El Salvador,
a plague commanded
by Camilo,
the King of Books.

con silencio estricto en el jeep,
dejándolo varado
sin dinero ni libros
en la frontera.

No lo persuadieron.
En su apartamento los libros se reproducen,
una infestación de libros,
apilándose, derramándose,
una horda de palabras impresas como saltamontes
ennegreciendo las pesadillas
de la policía de hacienda y capitanes del ejército
en El Salvador,
una plaga comandada
por Camilo,
el Rey de los Libros.

The Intelligence of Scavengers

Atlantic Coast of Nicaragua, 1982

Three vultures walk the ground clumsily
and hunch their wings
like renegade colonels
in rustling cloaks, in full-dress uniform.

They know the geography
of every ambush, the troop movements
of the mercenaries,
turning with an alert salute
of their beaks
to the many beckoning hands
of open graves.

The intelligence of scavengers
is everywhere in the countryside,
patiently scouting the moment
to skin the dead,
to parade arrogantly
among the living.

La inteligencia de los zopilotes

Costa Atlántica de Nicaragua, 1982

Tres buitres caminan por el suelo torpemente,
jorobando sus alas
como coroneles renegados
en capas que crujen, en uniforme de gala.

Conocen la geografía
de cada emboscada, los movimientos de tropa
de los mercenarios,
virándose con el saludo alerta
de sus picos
hacia las numerosas manos que les hacen señas
desde sus tumbas abiertas.

La inteligencia de los zopilotes
está por todo el campo,
pacientemente escrutinando hasta el momento
para despellejar a los muertos,
para desfilar con altivez
entre los vivos.

After the Flood in Chinandega

July, 1982

Nicaragua
is a young brown girl
standing in the mud
of a refugee camp,
grinning at the way
her green bird
balances himself
on her head

Después del diluvio en Chinandega

julio de 1982

Nicaragua
es una joven morena
de pie en el lodo
de un campamento para refugiados,
sonriéndose por la manera como
su pájaro verde
se equilibra
sobre su cabeza

For the Landlord's Repairman,
Since He Asked

Yes,
I am
one of those lawyers
who smuggles
Sandinistas
into the country

Para el obrero enviado por el casero, porque me lo preguntó

Sí,
soy
uno de esos abogados
que contrabandea
Sandinistas
para que se infiltren en el país

II.

To Skin the Hands of God

Para despellejar las manos de Dios

Federico's Ghost

The story is
that whole families of fruitpickers
still crept between the furrows
of the field at dusk,
when for reasons of whiskey or whatever
the cropduster plane sprayed anyway,
floating a pesticide drizzle
over the pickers
who thrashed like dark birds
in a glistening white net,
except for Federico,
a skinny boy who stood apart
in his own green row,
and, knowing the pilot
would not understand in Spanish
that he was the son of a whore,
instead jerked his arm
and thrust an obscene finger.

The pilot understood.
He circled the plane and sprayed again,
watching a fine gauze of poison
drift over the brown bodies
that cowered and scurried on the ground,
and aiming for Federico,
leaving the skin beneath his shirt
wet and blistered,
but still pumping his finger at the sky.

After Federico died,
rumors at the labor camp
told of tomatoes picked and smashed at night,
growers muttering of vandal children

El fantasma de Federico

Cuentan que
familias enteras de peones
aún se arrastraban entre los surcos
de los campos al anochecer,
cuando a raíz de whiskey o lo que sea
el avión regador roció de todas maneras,
dejando flotar una llovizna pesticida
sobre los que piscaban,
retorciéndose como pájaros oscuros
en una blanca red reluciente,
todos menos Federico,
un flaco joven de pie aparte
en su propio surco verde,
que a sabiendas de que el piloto
no comprendería en español
lo que era un hijo de puta,
sacudió su brazo
y lo embistió con un dedazo obsceno.

El piloto comprendió.
Hizo girar el avión y regó de nuevo,
mirando la fina gasa de veneno
esparcirse por encima de los cuerpos morenos
que se refugiaron y arrastraron por el suelo,
y haciéndole blanco a Federico,
dejándole la piel mojada y ampollada
por debajo de la camisa,
aún embistiendo su dedo hacia el cielo.

Después de que murió Federico,
los chismes en el campamento de trabajo
hablaban de tomates piscados y aplastados de noche,
terratenientes murmullando de niños vándalos

or communists in camp,
first threatening to call Immigration,
then promising every Sunday off
if only the smashing of tomatoes would stop.

Still tomatoes were picked and squashed
in the dark,
and the old women in camp
said it was Federico,
laboring after sundown
to cool the burns on his arms,
flinging tomatoes
at the cropduster
that hummed like a mosquito
lost in his ear,
and kept his soul awake.

o comunistas infiltrados,
primero amenazando con llamar a la Migra,
después prometiendo domingos sin trabajo
a cambio de que dejaran de machacar los tomates.

Pero los tomates seguían siendo piscados y aplastados
en la oscuridad,
y las ancianas del campamento
decían que era Federico,
trabajando después del anochecer
para calmar las quemaduras en sus brazos,
lanzándole tomates
al avión regador
que zumbaba como un mosquito
perdido en su oído,
manteniendo su alma despierta.

Nando Meets Papo

Somerset County, Maryland, August 1983

Nando was the one
from Legal Aid
who wore red suspenders
that spelled out
WORKER down one side
and SOLIDARITY
down the other,
biting like a watchdog
on a thin cigar,
with wild hair
and the dented-can grin
that made the landowners
in Somerset County
all sputter when he said
hola or hello.

He wasn't afraid of Papo either,
the cannonball-bellied crewleader
at Angelica
migrant labor camp,
even though Papo fired Shorty
for organizing,
then showed the chambers of his revolver
around camp,
boasting that any farmhand
who left the grounds
for the union or church
or to piss
could go al cielo
and tug at the robes of Jesus
that same day.

Nando conoce a Papo

Somerset County, Maryland, agosto de 1983

Nando era el
de Legal Aid
que vestía tirantes rojos
que deletreaban
SOLIDARIDAD por un lado
y OBRERA
por el otro,
mordiendo un cigarro delgado
como un perro guardián,
con pelo salvaje
y sonrisa de lata aplastada
que forzaba a todos los terratenientes
de Somerset County
tartamudear cuando les decía
hola o hello.

No le temía a Papo tampoco,
el capataz de panza como bala de cañón
en el campamento Angélica
de trabajadores migratorios,
aunque Papo había despedido a Shorty
por ser organizador,
mostrándole las cámaras de su revólver
por todo el campamento,
jactándose de que cualquier obrero
que dejara el campamento
para ir al sindicato o a la iglesia
o para mear
se iría al cielo
y jalaría la túnica de Jesús
el mismo día.

Nando chased Papo through town
in a red pickup truck
and caught him at the drugstore
to shove a court summons
down his stained white T-shirt;

the next time Nando
strutted through camp,
Papo sulked in the canteen
and the pickers applauded,
shirtless and laughing
like peasants drunk
at the landlord's wake,
conspiring union between beers,
welcomed back Shorty.

Nando persiguió a Papo por todo el pueblo
en una camioneta roja
y lo alcanzó en la farmacia
para meterle la orden para comparecer
por dentro de la blanca camiseta sucia;

la próxima vez que Nando
se pavoneó por el campamento,
Papo, refunfuñando, se refugió en la cantina
y los obreros aplaudieron,
descamisados y riéndose
como peones borrachos
en el velorio del terrateniente,
conspirando sindicalismo entre cervezas,
dándole la bienvenida de nuevo a Shorty.

Julio Signing His Name

Julio cheats
signing his name,
copying slowly
from his Social Security card,
man's hand
scratching letters child-crooked.

But Julio's black hand
was schooled for lettuce-picking,
not lawsuits.

Julio firmando su nombre

Julio hace trampa
al firmar su nombre,
copiándolo lentamente
de su tarjeta del Seguro Social,
la mano de un hombre
raspando letras torcidas de niño.

Pero la mano negra de Julio
la escolarizaron para piscar lechuga,
no para poner una demanda judicial.

The Florida Citrus Growers Association Responds to a Proposed Law Requiring Handwashing Facilities in the Fields

An orange,
squeezed on the hands,
is an adequate substitute
for soap and water

La Asociación de Productores de Cítricos de la Florida responde a un proyecto de ley requiriendo facilidades para lavarse las manos en los campos de trabajo

Una naranja,
exprimida sobre las manos,
es un sustituto adecuado
para agua y jabón

Justo the Painter and the Conquest of Lawrence

Lawrence, Massachusetts 1987

Shaking hands with us,
his palm is smooth
as seventy years' rain:
"El pintor primitivo dominicano
Justo Susana," he says,
bowing in a neat blue suit.
He poses with the painting
of Lawrence,
where he has not lived long enough
to learn hello
or the tricks of hiding
from immigration officers.

"Aquí 'tá Lawrence," he says,
tapping the painting:
burros grazing in the city park,
palm trees drooping over the highway,
bohío thatched huts sprouting
on the grounds of the factory,
and a brilliant sun, like fireworks
abolishing winter.

He will probably grin this way
when the government agents
escort him by the elbow
for deportation.
Let them.
Justo the painter has conquered Lawrence.

Justo el pintor y la conquista de Lawrence

Lawrence, Massachusetts 1987

Al darnos la mano,
su palma es lisa
como setenta años de lluvias:
"El pintor primitivo dominicano
Justo Susana", dice,
inclinándose en su nítido traje azul.
Posa con el cuadro
de Lawrence,
donde no ha vivido el tiempo suficiente
para aprender a decir hello
o las mañas para esconderse
de la Migra.

"Aquí 'tá Lawrence", dice,
tocando el cuadro:
burros pastando en el parque municipal,
palmeras languideciendo sobre la autopista,
bohíos floreciendo
alrededor de la fábrica,
y un sol brillante, como fuegos artificiales
aboliendo el invierno.

Probablemente se sonreirá de esta misma manera
cuando los agentes del gobierno
lo escolten del codo
para deportarlo.
Está bien.
Justo el pintor ya ha conquistado a Lawrence.

Jorge the Church Janitor Finally Quits

Cambridge, Massachusetts, 1989

No one asks
where I am from,
I must be
from the country of janitors,
I have always mopped this floor.
Honduras, you are a squatter's camp
outside the city
of their understanding.

No one can speak
my name,
I host the fiesta
of the bathroom,
stirring the toilet
like a punchbowl.
The Spanish music of my name
is lost
when the guests complain
about toilet paper.

What they say
must be true:
I am smart,
but I have a bad attitude.

No one knows
that I quit tonight,
maybe the mop
will push on without me,

Por fin renuncia Jorge el conserje de la iglesia

Cambridge, Massachusetts, 1989

Nadie me pregunta
de dónde soy,
tendré que ser
de la patria de los conserjes,
siempre he trapeado este piso.
Honduras, eres un campamento de desamparados
afuera de la ciudad
de su comprensión.

Nadie puede decir
mi nombre,
yo soy el amenizador
de la fiesta en el baño,
meneando el agua en el inodoro
como si fuera una ponchera.
La música española de mi nombre
se pierde
cuando los invitados se quejan
del papel higiénico.

Será verdad
lo que dicen:
soy listo,
pero tengo una mala actitud.

Nadie sabe
que esta noche renuncié al puesto,
quizá el trapero
seguirá adelante sin mí,

sniffing along the floor
like a crazy squid
with stringy gray tentacles.
They will call it Jorge.

husmeando el piso
como un calamar enloquecido
con fibrosos tentáculos grises.
Lo llamarán Jorge.

Moving Day in the Financial District

Boston, March 20, 1987

The moving crew began at 8 A.M.
The Anglos carried the smallest boxes
or snapped open beers
while the Puertorriqueños
hauled the metal desks,
the file cabinets, the shelves,
the work that shoved them grunting
down narrow stairs.

The landlord shouted
one-word commands
in all the Spanish he knew:
"!Aquí!"
"!Otro!"
and warned others away with,
"Let the guys do it."
On another floor, the Board meeting
was solemn behind glass doors,
soundproof.

Aguadilla is an early morning flight
no one can afford,
a pastel fantasy of the Caribbean Sea,
salvation dangling
beyond the hands
like a silver cross
slapping sweat
under the hard belly of a metal desk.

Día de mudanza en el distrito financiero

Boston, 20 de marzo de 1987

El equipo de mudanza comenzó su tarea a las 8 A.M.
Los anglos cargaban las cajas más pequeñas
o abrían cervezas
mientras los puertorriqueños
jalaban escritorios de metal,
los archiveros, las repisas,
el trabajo que los empujaba gruñendo
por las escaleras angostas.

El dueño gritaba
órdenes de una palabra
con todo el español que sabía:
"¡Aquí!"
"¡Otro!"
y advertía a los otros que se quitaran
con, "Deja que ellos lo hagan".
En otro piso la reunión de la junta directiva
solemne tras puertas de vidrio,
a prueba de sonido.

Aguadilla es un vuelo madrugador
que nadie puede pagar,
una fantasía de color pastel del Mar Caribe,
la salvación pendiendo
más allá del alcance
como un crucifijo de plata
azotando sudor
por debajo de la panza dura de un escritorio metálico.

The Secret of the Legal Secretary's Cigarette Smoke

for my mother

Cubicled women
pecking at computers,
observed by the senior partner
bowed and vigilant
as a gray monk,
watch in hand
at exactly 9 A.M.

Genuflection
to ashen priests of commerce,
bodies gliding in a hush
across the carpet
to leave coffee and pastries
for aristocratic hands
to contemplate.

At break time,
the senior partner's name
is a spat breath of cigarette smoke,
and even the quiet
religious woman
sneers.

El secreto del humo de cigarillo
de la secretaria legal

para mi madre

Mujeres en cubículos
rastreando computadoras,
observadas por el patrón mayor
agachado y vigilante como monje gris,
reloj en mano
exactamente a las 9 A.M.

Arrodillándose
ante curas cenicientos del comercio,
cuerpos deslizándose calladamente
por la alfombra
para dejarle café y pastelillos
a la contemplación
de manos aristocráticas.

A la hora del descanso,
el nombre del patrón mayor
es un aliento escupido
de humo de cigarillo,
y hasta la callada
mujer religiosa
hace una mueca desdeñosa.

The Words of the Mute are Like
Silver Dollars

Prince George's County, Maryland, 1976

Scrubbing cars for the factory showroom:
back pressed against the cool oily floor,
stink of the turpentine sponge,
radio sizzle, Maryland afternoon
cement-pale as the ceiling,
Ed the boss
leaning his cowboy face
over me.

"When I was in the Air Force,"
he said, "how come you Spanish greasers
always cut the lunch line?"
A picture of jostling metal trays,
brown soldiers accused
and paraded to the toilets
for the discipline of labor.

And so we are sprinkled with grease
and christened greaser: named
not for our hair and skin, as Ed
brave on beer would say,
but for the hours
we drag ourselves obediently
along his warehouse floor,
or whitening the urinals
in the barracks
with words for Ed
imprisoned in a cage of teeth, always
mute and stained as the sponge.

Las palabras de los mudos son como dólares de plata

Prince George's County, Maryland, 1976

Lavando carros en el salón de muestra de la fábrica,
espalda oprimida contra el piso fresco enaceitado,
hedor de terpentina esponjada,
el radio chispeando, una tarde de Maryland
pálida como el cemento del techo,
y el jefe Ed
inclinando su cara de vaquero
por encima de la mía.

"¿Cuando yo estaba en la Fuerza Aérea",
preguntó, "porqué era que ustedes Latinos grasosos
siempre cortaban la cola para almorzar?"
La imagen de bandejas metálicas golpeándose,
soldados morenos acusados
y enviados en desfile a limpiar los baños
como disciplina laboral.

Pues así nos riegan de grasa
y bautizan greasers: llamados así
no por nuestro pelo y nuestra piel, como diría Ed
con su valor encervezado,
sino por las horas
que nos arrastrábamos obedientemente
por el piso de su almacenaje,
o blanqueando los orinales
en los cuarteles
con palabras para Ed
encarceladas en una jaula de dientes, siempre
mudas y desteñidas como la esponja.

The words accumulate, stacked
like silver dollars in a box.
Brought from hiding,
they flash.

"Ed," I said, "how else
you get seconds
in America?"

Las palabras se acumulan, apiladas
como dólares de plata en una caja fuerte.
Brillan al sacarlas
de su escondite.

"¿Ed", dije, "y de qué otra manera
se logra comer bien
en los Estados Unidos?"

The Saint Vincent de Paul Food Pantry Stomp

Madison, Wisconsin, 1980

Waiting for the carton of food
given with Christian suspicion
even to agency-certified charity cases
like me,
thin and brittle
as uncooked linguini,
anticipating the factory-damaged cans
of tomato soup, beets, three-bean salad
in a welfare cornucopia,
I spotted a squashed dollar bill
on the floor, and with
a Saint Vincent de Paul food pantry stomp
pinned it under my sneaker,
tied my laces meticulously,
and stuffed the bill in my sock
like a smuggler of diamonds,
all beneath the plaster statue wingspan
of Saint Vinnie,
who was unaware
of the dance
named in his honor
by a maraca shaker
in the salsa band
of the unemployed.

Baileteo en el abastecimiento San Vicente de Paúl

Madison, Wisconsin, 1980

Esperando la caja de comida
regalada con Cristiana sospecha
hasta a casos de caridad debidamente certificados
como yo,
delgado y frágil
como linguini sin cocinar,
anticipando las latas dañadas
de sopa de tomate, remolacha, y ensalada a tres frijoles
en una cornucopia de welfare,
allí vi un dólar arrugado
sobre el piso, y con
un baileteo del abastecimiento de comida San Vicente de Paúl
lo atrapé por debajo de mi tenis,
amarré mis zapatos meticulosamente,
y metí el billete en mi media
como un contrabandista de diamantes,
todo por debajo de la estatua enyesada de brazos abiertos
de San Vicentico,
inconsciente
de la danza
nombrada en su honor
por un tocador de maracas
en la orquesta de salsa
de los desempleados.

Cusín and Tata

for my grandmother and my aunt
Río Piedras, Puerto Rico, 1988

Cusín waits for the white cruise ship,
iceberg-enormous, slicing
through the waters of San Juan,
and sells bargain gold
to the tourists,
greedy conquistadores in sunglasses.

Tata watches from the window
for her daughter
at Jardines del Paraíso
housing project,
hands in a knot
stitched tight by the repetition
of sewing machine years,
garment district factories
of women at tables
where the jabbing of the needle
becomes arthritis
shooting at the same speed.

Both have the Roig face,
a family of broad bones,
like the patriarch
in a photograph framed on the wall,
black suit
and children dressed in frills
at his feet.

The men are gone: the patriarch
lost in an unmarked grave,
Tata's gambler, generous with strangers,
husband who banned lipstick and the telephone,

Cusín y Tata

para mi abuela y mi tía
Río Piedras, Puerto Rico, 1988

Cusín espera el crucero blanco,
enorme como un iceberg, cortando su camino
por las aguas de San Juan,
y le vende oro barato
a los turistas,
conquistadores avaros en lentes de sol.

Tata vela por su hija
desde la ventana
en el caserío
Jardines del Paraíso,
manos enredadas
y tejidas por la repetición
de años costureros,
talleres de costura
de mujeres ante mesas
donde el pinchazo de la aguja
se vuelve artritis
disparando a la misma velocidad.

Ambos tienen la cara Roig,
una familia de huesos anchos,
como el patriarca
en una fotografía enmarcada en la pared,
traje negro
y niños vestidos de encaje
a sus pies.

Los hombres se han ido: el patriarca
perdido en una tumba sin lápida,
el jugador de Tata, generoso con desconocidos,
el esposo que le prohibía lápiz de labios y el teléfono,

who disappeared when his stiff command
was defied, once, and then gently.
Cusín's Paul slept in jail
when the first one was born,
a beer can fury
leaving the impression of his hand
in red streaks
across the skin of her memory.

Comes the hurricane
drowning the white ship,
comes the prediction
of Tata's only son
for two inches of blood in the gutter
and uprising's apocalypse
hailing over the island,

Tata and Cusín will stay
dry and tough
as the rice and beans in jars,
shuffling through snapshots
of Bronx-muffled children
in the winter of 1965
with another cup of café con leche.

y que se desapareció la única vez
que su orden inflexible fue desafiada, con suavidad.
Paul, él de Cusín, dormía en la cárcel
cuando nació el primero,
una furia de lata de cerveza
dejándole la impresión de su mano
en rayas rojas
a través de la piel de su recuerdo.

Llega el huracán
ahogando al barco blanco,
llega la predicción
del único hijo de Tata
de dos pulgadas de sangre
en la alcantarilla
y el apocalipsis del levantamiento
granizando sobre la isla,

Tata y Cusín se quedarán
secos y duros
como arroz y habichuelas en jarros,
barajando fotos
de niños abrigados del Bronx
en el invierno del 1965
con otra taza de café con leche.

To Skin the Hands of God

for Maynard Gilbert
Rocky Hill, Connecticut

The road that flattens
past the house
will always be known
by the family name.
Since 1680,
their lives
have been chopped and stacked
in a woodpile of work.
But once, with the gush
of a white river,
Gilbert Dairy fed
the distant city's
dry insatiable mouth,
and the family sat
in its own pew
at the church.

The squabbled inheritance,
the meticulous ledger
of grudges,
looting of shuttered bedrooms
after the burial,
and the price of milk
like the coins
in a beggar's grip:
the land sold to a cemetery
called Rose Hill,
the pond drained,
tombstones brushed
by the disappeared wisp
of cornstalks mowed down.

Para despellejar las manos de Dios

para Maynard Gilbert
Rocky Hill, Connecticut

La carretera que se aplasta
pasando por la casa
siempre será conocida
por su apellido.
Desde 1680,
sus vidas
han sido leños cortados y apilados
en una hoguera de trabajo.
Pero hace tiempo, con el brote
de un río blanco,
la Lechería Gilbert nutría
la insaciable boca seca
de la ciudad distante,
y la familia se sentaba
sobre su propio banco
en la iglesia.

La riña de herencia,
el meticuloso registro
de rencores,
el saqueo de alcobas cerradas
después del entierro,
y el precio de la leche
como las monedas
en el agarrón de manos de un mendigo:
la tierra vendida a un cementerio
llamado Rose Hill,
la charca drenada,
las lápidas rozadas
por los desaparecidos tallos
de maíz segado.

The family lived
by squirrel gun,
the chainsaw and the flask.

Now the father's paycheck
is signed
by the missile factory.
Tool and die,
cultivating the mathematical
perfection of warheads,
detonation's fragile craft.
Every five years, he says,
the missiles are scrapped,
unexploded, then reborn
in sleek new steel
by order of government contract.
Better this, he says,
than the truth
ostracized from the factory
like a failed union,
the certainty
of that blast
which will someday
skin the hands of God.

The tombstones in a half-moon
around his house
testify to the riches
in the marketplace of the dead,
the traders of the necropolis
shouting and bidding
for a dairy farmer's land and labor,
so that he wakes
too early for work, startled
at the hour of milking.

La familia vivía
de la pistola ardillera,
la motosierra y el frasco.

Ahora el cheque de pago del padre
lo firma
la fábrica de cohetes de guerra.
El fabricante de herramientas,
cultivando la perfección matemática
de cabezas explosivas,
la artesanía frágil de la detonación.
Cada cinco años, dice,
los cohetes son cancelados
sin explotar, luego renacidos
en nuevo acero reluciente
por orden del contrato gubernamental.
Mejor así, dice,
que la verdad
condenada al ostracismo de la fábrica
como un sindicato fracasado,
la certidumbre
de la explosión
que algún día
despellejará las manos de Dios.

Las lápidas en media luna
alrededor de su casa
rinden testimonio a las riquezas
en el mercado de los muertos,
los mercaderes de la necrópolis
gritando y apostando
por la tierra y la mano de obra de un lechero,
haciéndolo madrugar
a deshoras, espantado
a la hora del ordeño.

GLOSSARY

Spanish terms in original poems:

al cielo: to Heaven
aquí: here
barrio: Latino neighborhood
bohío: hut or shack
bolero: slow, romantic, often sad Latin American song and dance form
café con leche: coffee with steamed milk, as traditionally served in Puerto Rico and Cuba
colibrí: hummingbird
conga: tall drum of African origin
conquistadores: conquerors, usually referring to the Spanish
coro: chorus
Día de los Muertos: Day of the Dead, or All Souls day, especially as commemorated in México
duende: elf or goblin
fiesta: party
flamboyán: tree with red blossoms, common in Puerto Rico
Hernández: refers to the great Puerto Rican composer, Rafael Hernández
hijo de puta: son of a whore; sometimes translated as son of a bitch
Indio: Indian; refers here to Native American
jardines del paraíso: gardens of paradise
jíbaro: Puerto Rican term for peasant
maestro: master or teacher
mambo: Cuban song and dance form
Manteca: literally, "lard;" here, the name of a famous Afro-Cuban jazz composition by Chano Pozo and Dizzy Gillespie
negrito: literally, "little black one;" often used as a term of affection in Puerto Rico
otro: other or another
patrón: landowner or boss
pintor primitivo: primitivist painter

salsa: popular dance music which evolved in the Latino community
of New York during the 1960s
San Miguel: Saint Michael, the patron saint of Utuado, Puerto Rico
Taíno: the Indians of Puerto Rico, decimated by the Spanish
tecata: heroin
tumba: tomb or grave
Virgen de Guadalupe: mythical religious figure native to México,
representing a synthesis of Catholic and Indian religious beliefs

GLOSARIO

Términos puertorriqueños en las traducciones:

boricua: puertorriqueño; se refiere al nombre original de la isla
buscabulla: abusador o valentón
caserío: proyecto de vivienda para los pobres
conserje: portero
coquí: rana nativa de Puerto Rico, que canta por la noche
cotorra: loro pequeño
flamboyán: árbol de flores rojas, común en Puerto Rico
ganga: pandilla
guagua: autobús
Hernández: se refiere al gran compositor puertorriqueño, Rafael Hernández
jíbaro: campesino o peón
joseador: pícaro; persona de la calle
lagartijo: lagarto pequeño
Nacionalista: Partido Nacionalista; el movimiento pro-independencia más importante en la historia de Puerto Rico, especialmente durante los años treinta
pastelillo: pastel o pan dulce
pava: sombrero de paja, especialmente de los jíbaros
principal: director de la escuela
salsa: música popular bailable que se desarolló en la comunidad latina de Nueva York durante los años sesenta
taíno: los indios de Puerto Rico, diezmados por los españoles
tecata: heroína
yerba bruja: una clase de yerba mala encontrada en la región cafetalera de Puerto Rico

Biographical Notes

Puerto Rican poet **Martín Espada** was born in Brooklyn, New York in 1957. He is the author of two other books: *The Immigrant Iceboy's Bolero* (Waterfront Press) and *Trumpets From the Islands of Their Eviction* (Bilingual Press, Arizona State University). His poems have appeared in numerous journals and anthologies, including the *Agni Review, The Bilingual Review, Ploughshares, River Styx, An Ear to the Ground* (University of Georgia Press) and *Under 35: The New Generation of American Poets* (Doubleday/Anchor Books). He is also the editor of "Ten Poets: A Latino Supplement," in *Hanging Loose* magazine. He has been awarded a Massachusetts Artists Fellowship, a National Endowment for the Arts Creative Writing Fellowship, a Boston Contemporary Writers Award, the Open Voice Award, and the PEN/Revson Foundation Fellowship as well as the Paterson Poetry Prize for this volume.

Espada has been called "a rising star among the young Latino poets" in the Americas Review. In the Foreword to this book, Amiri Baraka writes, "There is an intensity of feeling here for the Puerto Rican people and culture, as well as the whole span of Latino...History, Culture, Life, that is deep-heavy, expressive; poignant, ironic, rollicking, bitter, revolutionary, tragic, by turns. As the poems' I turns, his self is touched by images the work delivers as if he had an amazing Polaroid Eye slung around his neck." PEN/Revson judges Carolyn Forché, Daniel Halpern, and Charles Simic were unanimous: "Whoever in the future wishes to find out the truth about our age will have to read poets like Martín Espada. He brings to American poetry an imagination and a sense of history which it has not previously known. The shared experience of Latin American immigrants and workers is his subject. This is political poetry at its best. These are poems about hard work and poverty and discrimination. He is the poet of that knowledge, the full weight of that knowledge. The greatness of Espada's art, like all great art, is that it gives dignity to the insulted and the injured of the earth."

Espada has worked as a radio journalist in Nicaragua, a welfare rights paralegal, a mental patient advocate, a night desk clerk in a transient hotel, an attendant in a primate nursery, a groundskeeper in a minor league ballpark, a bindery worker in a printing plant, and a bouncer in a bar, among other occupations. He currently lives in Boston, working as a tenant lawyer and supervisor of Su Clínica, a legal services program administered by Suffolk University Law School.

Translator, essayist, cultural organizer and civil rights lawyer, **Camilo Pérez-Bustillo** was born in Queens, New York, of Colombian parentage, in 1955. His work has appeared in such publications as *Hanging Loose, Hispanic, Left Curve,* the *Minnesota Review* and *Unity,* among others. His translation of essays by Juan Antonio Corretjer, entitled *Poetry and Revolution,* is forthcoming in the Curbstone Press Art on the Line series, and he is co-translator, with Martín Espada, of *Selected Poems* by Clemente Soto Vélez, also forthcoming from Curbstone Press. Pérez-Bustillo currently lives in San Francisco, where he works with Multicultural, Education, Training and Advocacy (META), Inc., a non-profit law firm specializing in bilingual education and the rights of linguistic and cultural minorities.

Other titles available from Curbstone

AFTER THE BOMBS, a novel by Arturo Arias, trans. by Asa Zatz. A lyrical documentation of the '54 coup in Guatemala, with zany humor and harsh insights into repression. $19.95cl. 0-915306-88-3; $10.95pa. 0-915306-89-1.

ASHES OF IZALCO, a novel by Claribel Alegría and Darwin J. Flakoll, trans. by Darwin J. Flakoll. A love story which unfolds during the bloody events of 1932, when 30,000 Indians and peasants were massacred in Izalco, El Salvador. $17.95cl. 0-915306-83-2; $9.95pa. 0-915306-84-0.

HAVE YOU SEEN A RED CURTAIN IN MY WEARY CHAMBER? selected writings by Tomás Borge; edited & trans. by Russell Bartley, Kent Johnson & Sylvia Yoneda. This first U.S. publication of Borge's poetry, essays and stories offers insight into this man, his work and the Nicaraguan Revolution. $9.95pa. 0-915306-81-6.

LUISA IN REALITYLAND, a prose/verse novel by Claribel Alegría; trans. by Darwin J. Flakoll. A retrospect of the real, surreal and magical memories of childhood in El Salvador into which the realities of war gradually intrude. $17.95 cl. 0-915306-70-0; $9.95 pa. 0-915306-69-7.

MIGUEL MARMOL, by Roque Dalton; trans. by Richard Schaaf. Long considered a classic testimony throughout Latin America, *Miguel Marmol* gives a detailed account of Salvadoran history while telling the interesting and sometimeshumorous story of one man's life. $19.95cl. 0-915306-68-9; $12.95pa. 0-915306-67-0.

TESTIMONY: Death of a Guatemalan Village by Victor Montejo; trans. by Victor Perera. *Testimony* gives an eyewitness account by a Mayan school teacher of an army attack on a Guatemalan village and its aftermath, told in a clean and direct prose style. $16.95cl. 0-915306-61-1; $8.95pa. 0-915306-65-4.

THE SHADOW BY THE DOOR by Gerardo di Masso; trans. by Richard Jacques. This novel takes place during the "dirty war" in Argentina and describes how a torture strives to maintain his sanity by recalling an adolescent love affair. $6.95pa. 0-915306-76-X.

FOR A COMPLETE CATALOG, SEND YOUR REQUEST TO:
Curbstone Press, 321 Jackson Street, Willimantic, CT 06226